Atomic Change

Learn the Habit to be successful and ways to get rid of the bad habit

Description

Atomic change are small, consistent, and incremental changes that are made in daily routines and behaviors. These habits are designed to help individuals achieve their goals and make lasting improvements in their lives. By focusing on the small and seemingly insignificant actions that are taken on a daily basis, atomic change aim to create a ripple effect that leads to larger, more significant changes over time. The idea behind atomic change is that by consistently making small improvements, individuals can develop the skills and behaviors needed to achieve their goals, without feeling overwhelmed or discouraged by the magnitude of the task at hand. Ultimately, atomic change are about creating a positive feedback loop of progress that leads to long-term success.

A short story of David

David had always struggled with procrastination and lacked the motivation to achieve his goals. One day, he stumbled upon the concept of atomic change, and it resonated with him. He realized that he needed to make small, consistent changes in his daily routines to achieve his long-term goals.

David decided to start small. He set a goal to wake up 30 minutes earlier each day and go for a quick run. He placed his running shoes and workout clothes next to his bed, so they were the first things he saw when he woke up in the morning. He also made sure to go to bed earlier, so he could get enough rest.

At first, it was difficult, and he struggled to wake up early. However, he kept at it and made sure to celebrate each small win. He noticed that he had more energy throughout the day and felt more productive at work.

After a few weeks, David added another small change to his routine. He decided to read for 15 minutes before going to bed each night. He placed a book on his nightstand, so it was easy to pick up and read.

As David continued to practice these small change, he noticed that they became easier to do, and he looked forward to them. He also realized that he had more time in the day and was able to accomplish more than before.

In time, David added more small change to his routine, such as drinking more water and taking short breaks throughout the day to stretch. Each small habit built upon the last, and he continued to make progress towards his long-term goals.

Through practicing atomic change, David was able to transform his daily routines and achieve his goals. He learned that small changes can make a big difference and that consistency is key.

About this book

There are lots of books about atomic change, these books has different names and also written by different author.

This books is a helpful book that has help so many people to become great in life, this book has the power to boost a lazy mindset into something great in life.

Being successful in life is a choice, the truth is everybody wants to be successful both lazy mindset and a non lazy mindset

I assure you that this book will help you achieve that greatness through some strategies you will be learning from this book, these strategies are 100% tested by great men and women

See you in the next state of becoming who you want to be and thank all the author for this wonderful book

Credit::::: Stephen. Jr. rechard

Table of contents

How your habit shapes your identity(chapter 1 to chapter 4):

Habits are things that we do without thinking much about them. They are routines that we have developed over time, and they shape who we are as individuals. Habits can be good or bad, and they have a significant impact on our daily lives. Our habits define us, and they shape our identity.

In this essay, we will explore the relationship between habit and identity. We will discuss how our habits shape our identity and how we can use habits to create a better version of ourselves. We will also explore how habits can be changed and how we can develop new habits that will help us reach our goals.

Chapter 1: The Relationship Between Habit and Identity

Habits are an essential part of our identity. They are the things that we do consistently, and they shape who we are as individuals. Habits can be good or bad, and they have a significant impact on our daily lives. Our habits define us, and they shape our identity.

When we think of our habits, we often think of the things that we do every day, such as brushing our teeth or taking a shower. However, habits go beyond just these routines. Habits also include the way we think, the way we interact with others, and the way we approach our goals.

Our habits are shaped by our environment, our upbringing, and our experiences. We develop habits over time, and they become a part of who we are. Our habits can be positive or negative, and they can have a significant impact on our lives.

Chapter 2: How Habits Shape Our Identity

Our habits shape our identity in many ways. They define who we are as individuals and influence the way we think, feel, and act. Our habits are the things that we do consistently, and they shape the way we approach our goals and challenges.

For example, if we have a habit of procrastination, it can have a significant impact on our lives. We may struggle to meet deadlines, and we may not be able to achieve our goals. On the other hand, if we have a habit of being organized and proactive, it can help us achieve our goals and reach our full potential.

Our habits also shape the way we interact with others. If we have a habit of being kind and empathetic, it can help us build strong relationships with others. However, if we have a habit of being negative and pessimistic, it can push people away and make it difficult for us to form meaningful connections.

Chapter 3: How to Develop Positive Habits

Developing positive habits is essential for shaping our identity. Positive habits can help us achieve our goals, build strong relationships, and improve our overall well-being. However, developing positive habits can be challenging, especially if we have been stuck in negative habits for a long time.

One way to develop positive habits is to start small. Instead of trying to change everything at once, focus on developing one positive habit at a time. For example, if you want to be more organized, start by making your bed every morning. Once you have developed this habit, move on to the next one.

Another way to develop positive habits is to create a routine. Set aside time each day to focus on developing your positive habits. For example, if you want to develop a habit of reading, set aside 30 minutes each day to read.

Chapter 4: How to Break Negative Habits

Breaking negative habits is just as important as developing positive habits.

How to build better Habit in 4 simple ways

Developing good habits is essential for achieving success in life. Habits are the small, daily actions that we take that shape our lives. They are the building blocks of our character, and they determine our level of success in life. In this essay, we will discuss four simple ways to build better habits.

Chapter 1: Start Small

One of the most effective ways to build better habits is to start small. When we try to make big changes in our lives, we often become overwhelmed and give up. By starting small, we can create momentum and build confidence.

For example, if you want to start exercising, start by taking a 10-minute walk each day. Once you have established this habit, gradually increase the length and intensity of your workouts.

Chapter 2: Make It Easy

Another way to build better habits is to make them easy to do. We are more likely to stick to habits that are easy and convenient. For example, if you want to drink more water, keep a water bottle with you at all times. If you want to read more, keep a book with you wherever you go.

Making habits easy to do also means removing obstacles that prevent us from doing them. For example, if you want to exercise in the morning, lay out your workout clothes the night before so that you are ready to go when you wake up.

Chapter 3: Use Positive Reinforcement

Positive reinforcement is a powerful tool for building better habits. When we reward ourselves for doing something, we are more likely to repeat that behavior. Rewards can be as simple as giving ourselves a pat on the back or as elaborate as treating ourselves to a special meal or activity.

For example, if you want to establish a habit of eating healthy, reward yourself with a small treat every time you choose a healthy meal. Over time, you will begin to associate healthy eating with positive feelings and will be more motivated to continue the habit.

Chapter 4: Track Your Progress

Tracking your progress is another effective way to build better habits. When we track our progress, we can see the results of our efforts and feel motivated to continue. Tracking can be as simple as marking off a calendar or as elaborate as using a habit tracking app.

For example, if you want to establish a habit of meditation, track the number of days that you meditate and the length of your meditation sessions. Seeing your progress will give you a sense of accomplishment and motivate you to continue the habit.

Conclusion:

Building better habits is a process that takes time and effort. By starting small, making habits easy, using positive reinforcement, and tracking progress, we can create lasting change in our lives. Building better habits is not always easy, but with persistence and dedication, we can achieve success and reach our full potential.

4 best way to start new habit

Starting a new habit can be challenging, but it is worth the effort. Habits can have a significant impact on our lives, affecting our health, productivity, and happiness. Whether you want to start exercising regularly, meditating daily, or reading more, there are many ways to make a new habit stick. In this article, we will explore four of the best ways to start a new habit and make it a part of your life.

1. Start Small and Build Momentum

One of the most effective ways to start a new habit is to start small and build momentum. Rather than trying to make a drastic change all at once, focus on making a small change that you can sustain. For example, if you want to start exercising regularly, start by committing to a 10-minute walk every day. This may not seem like much, but it is a small step in the right direction.

Once you have established the habit of daily walks, you can gradually increase the duration and intensity of your exercise. By starting small and building momentum, you are more likely to succeed in making the habit stick.

2. Make it a Part of Your Routine

Another effective way to start a new habit is to make it a part of your routine. We often have daily routines that we follow without even thinking about them. By incorporating your new habit into your existing routine, you are more likely to make it a part of your daily life.

For example, if you want to start meditating daily, try doing it first thing in the morning before you start your day. This will help you establish the habit and make it a natural part of your routine. Similarly, if you want to start reading more, try reading for 10 minutes before bed each night. By making your new habit a part of your routine, you are more likely to stick with it.

3. Use a Habit Tracker

A habit tracker is a simple tool that can help you stay motivated and accountable as you work to establish a new habit. A habit tracker can be as simple as a piece of paper or as complex as a digital app. The goal of a habit tracker is to help you track your progress and stay motivated.

To use a habit tracker, simply write down the habit you want to establish and track your progress each day. Seeing your progress visually can be a powerful motivator and can help you stay committed to your new habit.

4. Find an Accountability Partner

Finally, finding an accountability partner can be a powerful way to establish a new habit. An accountability partner is someone who shares your goal and can help you stay motivated and accountable as you work to establish the habit.

This can be a friend, family member, or even a professional coach. The key is to find someone who is supportive and can help you stay on track. By sharing your progress with someone else, you are more likely to stay committed to your goal and make the new habit a part of your life.

Conclusion

Starting a new habit can be challenging, but it is possible. By starting small, making it a part of your routine, using a habit tracker, and finding an accountability partner, you can increase your chances of success. Remember, it takes time and effort to establish a new habit, but the benefits are well worth it.

Motivation is overrated, Environment often matters more

Motivation is often seen as the key to success. We are often told that if we want to achieve our goals, we need to be motivated and driven. But the truth is, motivation is overrated. While it is important to have motivation, it is not the only factor that determines success. In fact, environment often matters more.

In this article, we will explore why motivation is overrated and how environment can play a more significant role in determining success. We will also discuss practical ways to create an environment that promotes success.

Why Motivation is Overrated:

Motivation is often seen as the key to success because it is what drives us to take action. When we are motivated, we are more likely to put in the effort required to achieve our goals. However, motivation is not always enough. There are several reasons why motivation is overrated:

1. Motivation is Fickle: Motivation is not a constant state. It can fluctuate depending on our mood, energy levels, and other external factors. This means that relying solely on motivation to achieve our goals is not a reliable strategy.

2. Motivation is Limited: Even when we are highly motivated, we can only sustain that level of motivation for a limited period of time. Eventually, our motivation will wane, and we will need to rely on other factors to keep us going.

3. Motivation is Not Enough: Even when we are highly motivated, there are often other factors that can derail our progress. For example, if we are trying to eat healthier, but we live in a food desert where healthy options are scarce, our motivation will be useless.

Why Environment Matters More:

While motivation is important, environment often matters more. Our environment includes the physical surroundings, the people we interact with, and the systems and structures that shape our lives. Here are some reasons why environment can be more important than motivation:

1. Environment Shapes Behavior: Our environment can influence our behavior in powerful ways. For example, if we live in a neighborhood where exercise is encouraged, we are more likely to be active. On the other hand, if we live in a neighborhood where crime is rampant, we are more likely to feel unsafe and avoid going outside.

2. Environment Provides Resources: Our environment can provide us with the resources we need to achieve our goals. For example, if we want to learn a new skill, we may need access to educational materials, mentors, and a supportive community. If we live in an environment that lacks these resources, it will be much harder to achieve our goals.

3. Environment Shapes Mindset: Our environment can also shape our mindset and beliefs. If we are surrounded by people who believe in us and encourage us, we are more likely to have a growth mindset and believe that we can achieve our goals. On the other hand, if we are surrounded by people who are negative and critical, we are more likely to have a fixed mindset and believe that we are limited in what we can achieve.

Creating an Environment for Success:

Now that we understand why environment matters more than motivation, let's explore some practical ways to create an environment that promotes success:

1. Surround Yourself with Positive Influences: Surround yourself with people who believe in you and encourage you. Seek out mentors and role models who can guide you and provide support.

2. Create a Supportive Community: Join a community of like-minded individuals who share your goals and values. This can be a group of friends

10 secret to self control

Self-control is a vital skill that can help us achieve our goals and lead fulfilling lives. Whether we want to improve our health, career, or relationships, self-control is essential to success. However, self-control is not always easy to master. It takes practice, discipline, and a willingness to make difficult choices.

In this article, we will explore 10 secrets to self-control that can help you develop this vital skill and achieve your goals.

1. Set Clear Goals:

The first secret to self-control is to set clear, specific goals. When we have a clear vision of what we want to achieve, it is easier to stay focused and motivated. Make sure your goals are realistic, achievable, and meaningful.

2. Develop a Plan:

Once you have set your goals, develop a plan for achieving them. Break your goals down into smaller, manageable steps and create a timeline for achieving each step. This will help you stay organized and on track.

3. Eliminate Distractions:

Distractions can be a major obstacle to self-control. Identify the things that distract you from your goals and eliminate them as much as possible. This may mean turning off your phone, avoiding social media, or creating a distraction-free workspace.

4. Build Habits:

Habits are powerful tools for self-control. When we develop positive habits, we can automate many of the choices that support our goals. Identify the habits that will help you achieve your goals and work to build them into your daily routine.

5. Practice Mindfulness:

Mindfulness is the practice of being present in the moment and aware of your thoughts and feelings. When we practice mindfulness, we can better control our impulses and make more intentional choices. Incorporate mindfulness practices like meditation or deep breathing into your daily routine.

6. Use Visualization:

Visualization is a powerful tool for self-control. When we visualize ourselves achieving our goals, we can increase our motivation and focus. Spend time each day visualizing yourself achieving your goals and experiencing the benefits that come with success.

7. Practice Self-Compassion:

Self-compassion is the practice of treating ourselves with kindness and understanding. When we practice self-compassion, we are less likely to be hard on ourselves when we make mistakes. Instead, we can learn from our mistakes and use them as opportunities for growth.

8. Get Enough Sleep:

Sleep is essential for self-control. When we are tired, it is harder to resist temptation and make good choices. Make sure you are getting enough sleep each night to support your self-control efforts.

9. Exercise:

Exercise is another key component of self-control. When we exercise, we release endorphins that boost our mood and increase our motivation. Exercise can also help us build physical and mental resilience, which is essential for self-control.

10. Seek Support:

Finally, seek support from others who share your goals and values. Join a support group, find a mentor, or seek guidance from a therapist. Having a supportive community can help you stay motivated and accountable as you work to develop self-control.

Conclusion:

Self-control is a vital skill that can help us achieve our goals and live fulfilling lives. By setting clear goals, developing a plan, eliminating distractions, building habits, practicing mindfulness, using visualization, practicing self-compassion, getting enough sleep, exercising, and seeking support, we can develop the self-control we need to succeed. Remember, self-control takes practice and discipline, but the rewards are well worth

How to make a Habit irresistible

Habits are the building blocks of our lives. They shape our behavior, determine our success, and contribute to our overall wellbeing. Habits are the things we do on autopilot, without even thinking about them. We form habits by repeatedly doing the same thing over and over again until it becomes second nature. Habits can be positive or negative and can have a profound impact on our lives. The key to making a habit irresistible is to create a strong enough desire to change and then to take small, consistent steps to make the change.

Chapter 1: Understanding Habits
Before we dive into the specifics of making habits irresistible, it's important to understand what habits are and how they work. Habits are behaviors that are repeated regularly and tend to occur subconsciously. They are formed by a cue, a routine, and a reward. The cue triggers the habit, the routine is the behavior itself, and the reward is the positive feeling or benefit that comes from completing the routine. Once a habit is formed, it becomes automatic and difficult to change.

Chapter 2: Identifying the Habits You Want to Change
The first step in making a habit irresistible is to identify the habits you want to change. Take some time to reflect on your current habits and identify which ones are holding you back or causing you harm. Once you have identified the habits you want to

change, write them down and be specific about what you want to change. For example, if you want to stop smoking, write down how many cigarettes you currently smoke per day and set a specific goal for how many you want to smoke per day or quit completely.

Chapter 3: Creating a Plan
Once you have identified the habits you want to change, it's time to create a plan. A plan will help you stay on track and make the necessary changes to your habits. Start by setting a specific goal for each habit you want to change. Be realistic and set goals that are achievable. For example, if you want to start exercising regularly, set a goal to exercise for 30 minutes a day, three times a week. Once you have set your goals, create a plan of action. Write down the steps you need to take to achieve your goals, and be sure to break them down into manageable tasks.

Chapter 4: Creating a Strong Desire to Change
Creating a strong desire to change is essential if you want to make your habits irresistible. Without a strong desire to change, it's unlikely that you will be successful in changing your habits. One way to create a strong desire to change is to identify the benefits of changing your habits. For example, if you want to start eating healthier, identify the benefits of eating healthy such as having more energy, feeling better, and reducing your risk of disease.

Chapter 5: Making Small, Consistent Changes

Making small, consistent changes is the key to making your habits irresistible. It's important to start small and gradually increase the difficulty of the habit. For example, if you want to start exercising regularly, start by exercising for 10 minutes a day and gradually increase the time each week. Consistency is also important. Make a commitment to yourself to do the habit every day, even if it's only for a few minutes. Over time, the small changes will add up, and the habit will become easier to maintain.

The role of family and friends in shaping your habit

Habits are a fundamental part of our daily lives. They shape our behavior, determine our success, and contribute to our overall wellbeing. Habits can be positive or negative and can have a profound impact on our lives. Family and friends play a critical role in shaping our habits. They influence our behavior, provide support, and help us stay accountable. In this article, we will explore the role of family and friends in shaping our habits and how we can leverage their support to create positive change in our lives.

Chapter 1: The Power of Social Influence
Humans are social creatures, and we are wired to seek the approval and support of others. This social influence can play a significant role in shaping our habits. We are more likely to adopt the habits of those around us, whether they are positive or negative. For example, if our family and friends smoke, we are more likely to smoke as well. On the other hand, if our family and friends exercise regularly, we are more likely to adopt that habit as well.

Chapter 2: The Importance of Support
Support from family and friends can be a powerful motivator when trying to create new habits. Having a support system can provide encouragement, accountability, and motivation to stick to our goals. This support can come in many forms, such as joining us in our new habit, providing words of

encouragement, or simply being there to listen and offer guidance.

Chapter 3: Creating a Positive Environment
Creating a positive environment is essential when trying to create new habits. Our environment can influence our behavior and make it easier or harder to maintain our habits. Family and friends can play a critical role in creating a positive environment. For example, if we want to eat healthier, our family and friends can support us by cooking healthy meals, choosing healthy restaurants, and avoiding junk food around us.

Chapter 4: Overcoming Resistance from Family and Friends
Sometimes, family and friends can be resistant to our new habits. They may not understand why we want to change or may not be supportive of our goals. It's important to remember that their resistance is not necessarily a reflection of us or our goals. It may be a reflection of their own fears or insecurities. It's important to communicate our goals clearly and explain why they are important to us. We can also try to find common ground and compromise where possible.

Chapter 5: Leveraging Technology and Social Media
Technology and social media can be powerful tools for creating and maintaining new habits. We can use technology to track our progress, set reminders, and connect with others who share our goals. We can also use social media to share our progress and get support

from others. Family and friends can play a critical role in this process by following us on social media, commenting on our progress, and providing encouragement.

Chapter 6: Maintaining Accountability
Accountability is essential when trying to create new habits. We need to hold ourselves accountable for our actions and stay committed to our goals. Family and friends can play a critical role in this process by holding us accountable, checking in on our progress, and providing feedback. We can also enlist the help of a coach or mentor to provide additional support and guidance.

Conclusion:

Family and friends play a critical role in shaping our habits. They influence our behavior, provide support, and help us stay accountable. By leveraging their support, we can create positive change in our lives and achieve our goals. We must remember that change can be difficult

How to find and fix the causes of your bad habit

Habits can be powerful tools for achieving our goals and improving our lives. However, not all habits are positive, and some can have a negative impact on our wellbeing. Bad habits can be difficult to break, but it's essential to identify and address the root causes of the habit if we want to make lasting change. In this article, we will explore how to find and fix the causes of your bad habit, so you can create positive change in your life.

Chapter 1: Understanding the Nature of Habits
Before we dive into the specifics of finding and fixing the causes of bad habits, it's important to understand the nature of habits. Habits are behaviors that are repeated regularly and tend to occur subconsciously. They are formed by a cue, a routine, and a reward. The cue triggers the habit, the routine is the behavior itself, and the reward is the positive feeling or benefit that comes from completing the routine. Once a habit is formed, it becomes automatic and difficult to change.

Chapter 2: Identifying Your Bad Habit
The first step in finding and fixing the causes of your bad habit is to identify the habit itself. Take some time to reflect on your behavior and identify which habits are holding you back or causing harm. Once you have identified the bad habit, write it down and be specific about what you want to change.

Chapter 3: Examining the Cue
The cue is the trigger that sets off the habit. To find and fix the causes of your bad habit, you need to examine the cue and determine what is triggering the behavior. The cue can be anything, such as a time of day, a specific location, or a particular emotion. Once you have identified the cue, you can start to make changes to your environment or routine to remove or alter the trigger.

Chapter 4: Examining the Routine
The routine is the behavior itself, and it's essential to examine it to find and fix the causes of your bad habit. Look at the behavior objectively and try to identify what is driving it. Is it a coping mechanism for stress or anxiety? Is it a way to seek pleasure or avoid pain? Once you understand the motivation behind the behavior, you can start to make changes to your routine to address the underlying cause.

Chapter 5: Examining the Reward
The reward is the positive feeling or benefit that comes from completing the routine. It's important to examine the reward to find and fix the causes of your bad habit. Identify what you are gaining from the behavior and whether it's worth the negative consequences. If the reward is not worth the negative consequences, you can start to look for alternative behaviors that provide a similar reward without the negative consequences.

Chapter 6: Making Changes to Your Environment and Routine

Once you have identified the cue, routine, and reward, you can start to make changes to your environment and routine to address the underlying causes of your bad habit. For example, if you have a bad habit of eating junk food when you're stressed, you can try to remove the junk food from your environment and replace it with healthier options. You can also try to find alternative ways to cope with stress, such as exercise or meditation.

Chapter 7: Seeking Support and Accountability
Breaking a bad habit can be challenging, and it's essential to seek support and accountability to stay on track. This support can come from friends, family, or a coach or mentor. They can provide encouragement

How to stick with good habits everyday

Developing good habits is an essential part of achieving success in any area of life. Whether it's for personal growth, career advancement, or physical fitness, the ability to establish and maintain positive habits is a crucial skill to have. Unfortunately, many people struggle with sticking to their good habits, often falling back into old patterns and routines. In this guide, we'll explore the science behind habit formation and provide practical tips and strategies for sticking with good habits every day.

Chapter 1: Understanding Habits

Before we dive into strategies for sticking with good habits, it's essential to understand what habits are and how they work. A habit is a learned behavior that becomes automatic over time. In other words, it's something you do without even thinking about it. Habits can be positive or negative, and they often form as a result of repetition and reinforcement.

The science behind habit formation involves a feedback loop that consists of three stages: the cue, the routine, and the reward. The cue is a trigger that initiates the habit, the routine is the behavior itself, and the reward is the positive reinforcement that reinforces the habit. By understanding this feedback loop, you can begin to identify the cues and rewards associated with your habits and modify them to create positive change.

Chapter 2: Setting Goals

The first step in sticking with good habits is to set clear, specific goals. Without a clear goal in mind, it's easy to become distracted or lose motivation. When setting goals, it's essential to make them SMART: specific, measurable, achievable, relevant, and time-bound. For example, instead of setting a goal to "exercise more," make it specific by saying, "I will exercise for 30 minutes every day." This makes the goal measurable and achievable, and it's relevant to your overall health and fitness goals.

Chapter 3: Start Small

One of the most common mistakes people make when trying to establish new habits is trying to do too much too soon. Starting small is essential when developing new habits because it helps to build momentum and create a sense of accomplishment. Instead of trying to make significant changes all at once, focus on making small, incremental changes. For example, if your goal is to read more, start by reading for just five minutes each day and gradually increase the time as you become more comfortable.

Chapter 4: Create a Routine

One of the most effective ways to stick with good habits is to create a routine. A routine is a set of actions or behaviors that you do consistently at the same time each day. By creating a routine, you're making it easier to perform the habit because it becomes a natural part of your daily routine. For example, if your goal is to meditate each morning, create a routine that involves waking up at the same time each day, meditating for a set amount of time, and then starting your day.

Chapter 5: Eliminate Distractions

Distractions can derail even the best-laid plans. To stick with good habits, it's essential to eliminate distractions as much as possible. This might mean turning off your phone during certain times of the day, closing your office door, or finding a quiet space to work. By eliminating distractions, you're creating an environment that's conducive to focusing on your habits and achieving your goals.

How to stay motivated in life and work

Motivation is the driving force behind achieving our goals and living a fulfilling life. Whether it's at work or in our personal lives, staying motivated can make the difference between success and failure. However, maintaining motivation is not always easy. In this guide, we will explore the science behind motivation and provide practical strategies for staying motivated in life and work.

Chapter 1: Understanding Motivation

Before we dive into strategies for staying motivated, it's essential to understand what motivation is and how it works. Motivation is defined as the internal or external factors that drive behavior toward a particular goal. There are two types of motivation: extrinsic and intrinsic. Extrinsic motivation comes from external factors, such as rewards or punishments, while intrinsic motivation comes from within, such as personal satisfaction or a sense of purpose.

The science behind motivation involves the brain's reward system, which releases dopamine when we achieve a goal or receive a reward. This dopamine release creates a positive feeling that drives us to continue pursuing our goals. Understanding this system can help us harness the power of motivation and stay on track.

Chapter 2: Setting Goals

The first step in staying motivated is setting clear, specific goals. Without a goal in mind, it's easy to become distracted or lose motivation. When setting goals, it's essential to make them SMART: specific, measurable, achievable, relevant, and time-bound. For example, instead of setting a goal to "get in shape," make it specific by saying, "I will run three miles each day for the next month."

Chapter 3: Finding Purpose

Finding purpose is an essential factor in staying motivated. When we have a clear sense of purpose, we are more likely to stay motivated and focused on our goals. To find purpose, ask yourself what is important to you and what brings you fulfillment. This might involve volunteering, pursuing a passion project, or finding meaning in your work.

Chapter 4: Creating a Routine

Creating a routine is a powerful way to stay motivated. When we establish a routine, we are more likely to follow through with our goals because they become a natural part of our daily routine. For example, if your goal is to exercise each morning, create a routine that involves waking up at the same time each day, exercising for a set amount of time, and then starting your day.

Chapter 5: Building Momentum

Building momentum is another important factor in staying motivated. When we achieve small wins, we build momentum and are more likely to continue pursuing our goals. To build momentum, break down your goals into smaller, achievable steps. Celebrate each small win along the way, and use that positive energy to fuel your motivation.

Chapter 6: Staying Accountable

Accountability is a crucial component of staying motivated. When we are accountable to someone else, we are more likely to follow through with our goals. This might involve finding a workout partner, joining a support group, or working with a coach or mentor.

Chapter 7: Overcoming Obstacles

Obstacles are inevitable on the path to achieving our goals. However, how we respond to these obstacles can make all the difference. To overcome obstacles, identify the problem, brainstorm possible solutions, and take action. Remember that setbacks are not failures, but opportunities to learn and grow.

Chapter 8: Fostering a Growth Mindset

Finally, fostering a growth mindset is essential in staying motivated. A growth mindset involves believing that our abilities and intelligence can be.

Appreciation

I want to take a moment to express my sincerest gratitude for taking the time to read this book. Thank you for sticking with it until the very end. I know that reading a book can be a significant investment of time and energy, and I am truly honored that you chose to spend that time with me.

As an author, there is nothing more gratifying than knowing that someone has read and appreciated your work. Writing a book is a labor of love, and it's incredibly rewarding to see that work resonate with readers. Your support means the world to me, and I couldn't be more grateful.

I hope that this book has provided you with value, insight, and inspiration. My ultimate goal in writing it was to help you in some way, whether it's by providing practical advice, sharing personal experiences, or simply offering a new perspective.

I know that reading is a personal experience, and everyone takes something different away from a book. If this book has helped you in any way, I would love to hear about it. Please feel free to write a review and share your thoughts and feedback.

Once again, thank you for your support and for taking the time to read this book. Your commitment and dedication are truly appreciated. I hope that this book has been a positive and meaningful experience for

you, and I wish you all the best in your journey ahead.
Also check out my page for helpful books too, I wrote lots of new books that are helpful to both kids and adults, go check it out on my page.

Thank you All